DOUBLE

MW00527336

MEASURES *of* SUCCESS®
for string orchestra
A Comprehensive Musicianship String Method

GAIL V. BARNES • BRIAN BALMAGES • CARRIE LANE GRUSELLE • MICHAEL TROWBRIDGE

Congratulations on completing the first book of *Measures of Success®* and welcome to Book 2! Throughout this book, you will explore music from many different countries around the world and learn about many composers that you did not encounter in Book 1. You will also explore some of the fascinating historical events that help bring the days of these composers to life.

Enjoy this exciting time in your musical growth. As you practice, you will continue to find yourself sharing the gift of music with family, friends and audiences.

Ready?

Let's make music!

ALL-IN-ONE DVD

Your book comes with an All-in-One DVD. It includes tuning notes, instructional videos, and accompaniments for every exercise in the book. You can also put the DVD into your computer to access and transfer the mp3 files to a portable device or burn to a CD. You may also access all videos and recordings online by visiting www.fjhmusic.com/downloads and entering the following authentication code. It's that easy!

Website: www.fjhmusic.com/downloads
Authentication Code: 52232893476

Recording Credits
Arrangements by Brian Balmages, Ryan Fraley, and Ralph Johnson
Recorded at The Lodge Recording Studios; Indianapolis, IN
Executive Producer: Brian Balmages

Producer: Ryan Fraley • Engineer: Michael Graham
Programming: Ryan Fraley and Ralph Johnson
Label Design: Andi Whitmer

Production: Frank J. Hackinson
Cover Design: Danielle Taylor and Andi Whitmer
Interior Line Drawings: Adrianne Hirosky, Danielle Taylor, and Andi Whitmer
Interior Layout and Design: Andi Whitmer
Production Coordinator: Brian Balmages
Printer: Tempo Music Press, Inc.

ISBN-13: 978-1-61928-128-8

PRELUDE HARMONICS

A **prelude** is a piece of music that introduces a larger work. In this case, the prelude is a way to loosen your left hand before you begin playing the music in Book 2. Refer to this page often and use it as part of your daily practice routine.

VIDEO

HARMONICS

A **harmonic** occurs when you touch the string lightly with your 3rd finger, resulting in a higher pitched note. To play the harmonics below, place your 3rd finger exactly in the middle of the string, splitting it into two equal lengths from the nut to the bridge. While lightly touching the string, use a good amount of bow speed and bow pressure to help the note sound. You should hear a note one octave higher than your open string. Harmonics played on open strings are called **natural harmonics**. Keep your left hand loose and flexible as you move up and down the fingerboard!

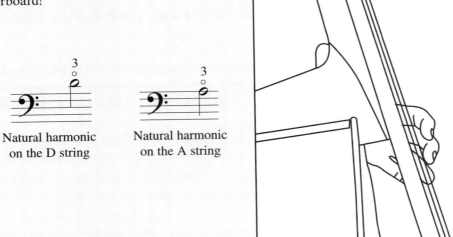

Natural harmonic on the D string   Natural harmonic on the A string

As you move your hand, your thumb will stop at the end of the neck. Expand your hand so the finger reaches the correct spot on the string!

Prelude 1: MOVING AROUND *Are your harmonics in tune with your open strings? Be sure they have a strong, ringing tone!*

Prelude 2: UP AND DOWN *Keep your left hand relaxed and flexible as you move up and down the fingerboard.*

Prelude 3: CLIMBING MOUNT EVEREST *Your thumb should also move, staying relaxed and behind your 2nd finger.*

Prelude 4: FLOATING

Prelude 5: SMOOTH SLIDER *Notice the left-hand pizzicato in the last measure.*

OPUS 1

3

D MAJOR REVIEW

1.1 LOOSEY-GOOSEY *Keep your bow arm relaxed and focus on making a great tone!*

1.2 THE DANCING TETRACHORD

1.3 TUNING TUNE - Duet *Is the A part in tune with the open strings in the B part?*

1.4 IN TUNE NATION - Duet

1.5 ORANGES AND LEMONS

English Folk Song

1.6 EARLY TO BED - Round

American Folk Song

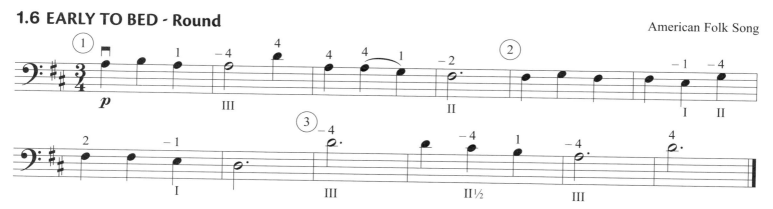

SB308DB

DETACHÉ

A **detaché** bow stroke is often used in music where the performer is required to play multiple notes of similar value that are smooth and connected. Use one broad stroke per note!

Unlike the term *legato,* which refers to an entire passage, *detaché* refers to a bow stroke used on specific notes within a passage.

1.7 DETACHÉ SASHAY *Use a detaché bow stroke for all eighth notes in this piece.*

STACCATO

Unlike *detaché,* **staccato** notes are short and separated.
Play staccato by stopping the bow between each note.

1.8 D MAJOR ROMP *Notice how this piece uses detaché eighth notes and staccato quarter notes. Look out for the left-hand pizzicato in the last measure!*

G MAJOR REVIEW

1.9 GROOVIN' IN G

1.10 CRIPPLE CREEK

Appalachian Folk Song

SLURS AND TIES

Remember that a **tie** connects notes of the **same pitch.**
A **slur** connects notes of **different pitches.**
All notes in a tie or slur are played **using a single bow.**

1.11 BOW TIES AND SLURS

1.12 SUR LE PONT D'AVIGNON

French Folk Song

Moderato

1.13 CAPRICCIO ITALIEN
Use a light and fast up bow after each half note. This will prevent the quarter notes from sounding heavy and loud.

Pyotr I. Tchaikovsky

Allegro

HISTORY

MUSIC
German composer **Johannes Brahms** (1833–1897) was also an accomplished violist and pianist. He gave the first performance of many of his own works. His *Symphony No. 1* for orchestra is less than an hour long, yet it took him nearly 21 years to complete!

LITERATURE
The same year Brahms completed his first symphony, Mark Twain finished his novel *The Adventures of Tom Sawyer*. The story portrays the life of a young boy growing up along the Mississippi River.

WORLD
The first official National League Baseball Game was played and the first telephone call was made. Things got fishy in Maine when sardines were canned for the first time!

1.14 THEME FROM SYMPHONY NO. 1
Use a fast, light up bow in the first ending. This will prevent the D from sounding much louder than the rest of the melody!

Johannes Brahms

Moderato

HISTORY

Hildegard von Bingen (ca. 1098 - 1179) was a female German composer who also made substantial contributions as a philosopher and writer.

1.15 CARITAS ABUNDAT ("Charity Abounds")

Hildegard von Bingen

Andante

1.16 HOPPING UP AND GLIDING DOWN

Allegro

SB308DB

C MAJOR REVIEW

1.17 KEY OF C, SEE?

1.18 IFCA'S CASTLE - Round
Use a slower bow on dotted half notes and a faster, lighter bow on quarter notes.

Czech Folk Song

1.19 THIS OLD MAN
Remember to use 2nd finger on the D and A strings when playing in the key of C Major.

English Folk Song

Moderato

1.20 CHORALE - Duet
In the A line, prepare finger 2 for the second note.
In the B line, prepare finger 1 for the second note.

Andante

1.21 LONG, LONG AGO

Thomas Haynes Bayly

Andante

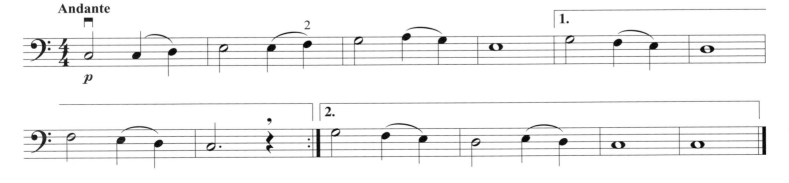

SIXTEENTH NOTES

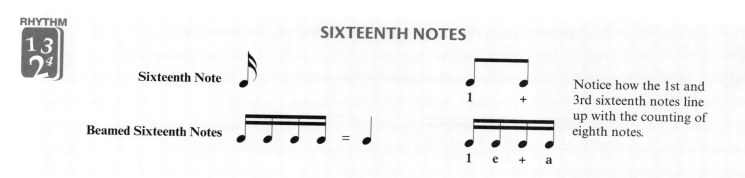

Sixteenth Note

Beamed Sixteenth Notes

Notice how the 1st and 3rd sixteenth notes line up with the counting of eighth notes.

1.22 BOW BEAT *Rosin bow, then play on an open string. Play with detaché bow strokes and stay in the middle of the bow. Be sure you are opening your arm from the elbow.*

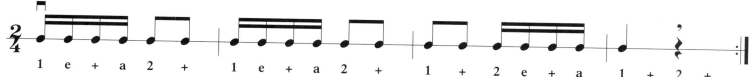

1.23 16th STREET *Use a detaché bow stroke on the sixteenth notes.*

1.24 BOW-DACIOUS *Continue refining your detaché bow stroke!*

1.25 MAYBE NEXT TIME

1.26 FROGGIE WENT A-COURTIN' *Remember to keep counting when playing half notes that are tied to quarter notes!*

English Folk Song

SB308DB

RHYTHM 13

EIGHTH NOTE/TWO SIXTEENTH NOTE GROUP

An eighth note can replace the first two sixteenth notes in a group of four sixteenth notes.
This creates an **eighth note/two sixteenth note group.**

1.27 BOW BEAT *Use shorter bow strokes on sixteenth notes and longer bow strokes on eighth notes.*
Use the slowest bow for quarter notes.

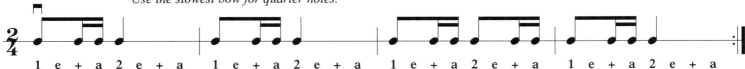

1.28 SIXTEEN FIDDLES!

1.29 TELL WILLIAM ABOUT HIS OVERTURE

Adaptation of Rossini

1.30 THE MATADOR *Start with your bow at the balance point. Use a small amount of bow on notes before bow lifts.*

1.31 PERPETUAL MOTION

RHYTHM

TWO SIXTEENTH NOTE/EIGHTH NOTE GROUP

An eighth note can replace the last two sixteenth notes in a group of four sixteenth notes.
This creates a **two sixteenth note/eighth note group.**

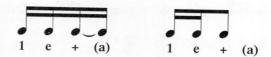

1.32 BOW BEAT

1.33 HERE WE BOW AGAIN

1.34 STODOLA PUMPA

Czech Folk Song

1.35 SOMEONE'S IN THE KITCHEN...

Start in the middle of the bow so you have enough bow for measure 2.

J. H. Cave

1.36 JIM ALONG JOSIE

American Folk Song

OPUS 1 ENCORE

INTERPRETATION STATION

Listen to the corresponding track on the DVD. You will hear a tempo given by a click track. This is the speed of a quarter note. You will then hear a rhythm. Select which notated rhythm is being played and write the corresponding answer letter on the line. Each example is performed twice.

1. _____   3. _____

2. _____   4. _____

SIMON SEZ

Listen to the corresponding track on the DVD. You will hear a series of 1-measure patterns. Listen to the patterns and echo them back. *Hint: the first pattern starts on your open D string!*

COMPOSER'S CORNER

Many composers use key changes to make a piece more interesting. Rewrite the first two measures in the key of G Major, using the notes in measure 3 as a guide. When finished, play the entire piece!

PENCIL POWER

Match each definition with its correct term by writing in the appropriate letter.

1. _____ D Major   5. _____ Staccato

2. _____ Tie   6. _____ Slur

3. _____ Détaché   7. _____ *piano*

4. _____ C Major   8. _____ G Major

A. Key signature with no sharps
B. Italian term which means to play softly
C. Key signature with 1 sharp
D. Play short and separated
E. Connects notes of different pitches
F. Play smooth and connected using one broad stroke per note
G. Key signature with 2 sharps
H. Connects notes of the same pitch

CURTAIN UP!

Time to perform! The following music showcases what you have learned in Opus 1.

1.37 BARN DANCE!

BOW-NUS!

Demonstrate a relaxed left hand as you play this piece that uses harmonics.

1.38 PHIL-HARMONICS

CURTAIN UP!

1.39 MOTO PERPETUO - Orchestra Arrangement

Brian Balmages

OPUS 2

BOW SPEED

Bow speed management and control are an essential part of developing right-hand technique and a musical sound. In the following exercises, you will be required to use a very fast bow on certain quarter notes. In order to keep those notes from sounding a lot louder, practice using a lighter bow stroke in combination with the faster bow movement.

2.1 LIGHT RAIL *Use a light, fast bow on quarter notes so they do not sound any louder than dotted half notes!*

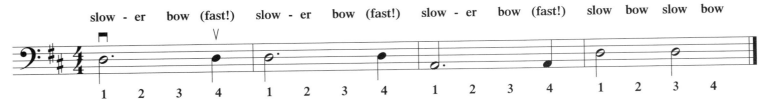

2.2 SHE WORE A YELLOW RIBBON *Think about bow speed and weight before playing this piece!* Traditional American

2.3 MINUET - Duet *Use a fast, light bow on quarter notes that follow a half note in 3/4 time!* Daniel G. Türk

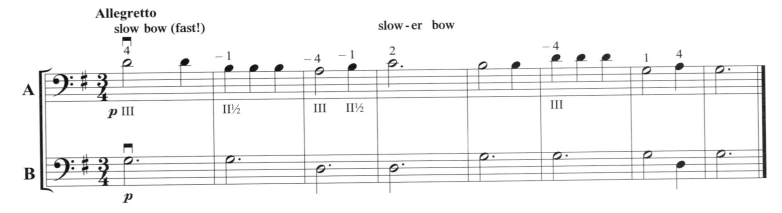

2.4 GOOD NIGHT LADIES *Check your key signature so you know whether the Fs are sharp or natural! Use a fast, light bow on the quarter notes in measures 2 and 4.* Traditional

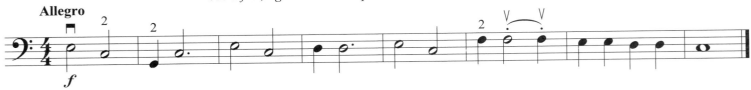

2.5 SPEED ZONE

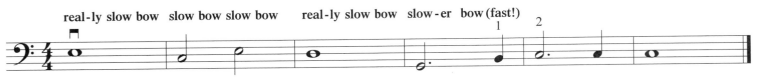

RHYTHM 13 2.4

RETURN OF THE DOT RULE

Adding a dot after a note increases the length of the note by half its value. Here, the dot is used with a quarter note to create a **dotted quarter note**.

2.6 BOW BEAT

quar-ter eighth eighth   quar-ter tie eighth   quar-ter dot eighth

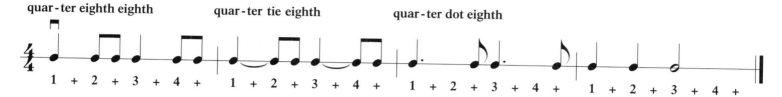

2.7 BACKWARD DOT POLKA *Use a light, fast bow on eighth notes so they do not sound any louder than dotted quarter notes!*

quar-ter tie eighth   quar-ter dot eighth

2.8 DOTS A LOT

THEORY

DYNAMICS

Mezzo is an Italian term that means "medium" or "moderately." The letter *m* is an abbreviation used in dynamics.

mp (*mezzo piano*) – moderately soft   *mf* (*mezzo forte*) – moderately loud

2.9 ALOUETTE *Think about bow speed and weight before playing this piece.*

French-Canadian Folk Song

2.10 TUR-BOW *Focus on your right-hand technique as you practice these rhythm combinations on your open strings.*

2.11 RHYTHM MASHUP!

SB308DB

2.12 FULL STRING AHEAD! (FIGHT SONG) - DUET

2.13 OVER SMOOTH SEAS *Slow your bow speed so that you are able to play all the rhythms with the correct value.*

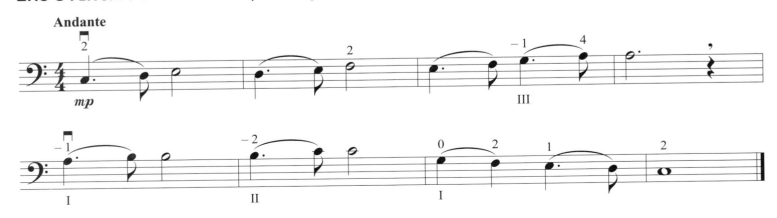

BOW DISTRIBUTION

In addition to bow speed, **bow distribution** is an essential part of developing right-hand technique. Look at the picture and then at your own bow. Experiment with putting the bow on an open string and play quarter notes while isolating each part of the bow as illustrated below.

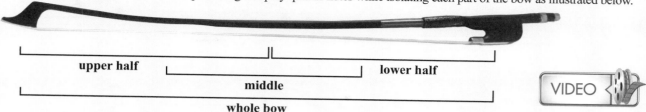

VIDEO

2.14 LEAP FROG *Play this piece using only the lower half of the bow.*

2.15 TIP TOE *Play this piece using only the upper half of the bow.*

2.16 MIDDLE GROUND *Stay in the middle of the bow while playing this piece.*

THEORY

NEW KEY SIGNATURE

This is the key of **F Major**.

♭ The **flat sign** lowers a pitch by a half step.

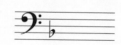

This key indicates that all Bs should be played as B-flat. Even though you have not learned B♭ yet, you will be practicing in the key of F Major, which will help you when you learn B♭ later in this Opus!

HISTORY

MUSIC
Antonín Dvořák (1841–1904) was a Czech composer who often used elements of native folk music in his compositions. His *Symphony No. 9* ("*From the New World*") was written when he was living in New York and was premiered by the New York Philharmonic.

LITERATURE
Scottish writer Sir Arthur Conan Doyle introduced the world to Sherlock Holmes in a mystery novel entitled *A Study in Scarlet*. Holmes and his friend, Dr. John Watson, went on to become two of the most recognized names in literature.

WORLD
Yellowstone became the first national park in the United States. This marked the first time that the federal government made a specific effort to preserve parts of the western wilderness.

2.17 LARGO FROM SYMPHONY NO. 9 *Using a full bow will help you play at a slower tempo.*

Antonín Dvořák

2.18 AULD LANG SYNE

Traditional

2.19 SEA CHANTEY - Duet   *Switch parts on the repeat!*

Traditional Melody

2.20 THREE IN ONE   *Practice playing three notes in one bow.*

HISTORY

MUSIC

Norwegian composer **Edvard Grieg** (1843–1907) was also an accomplished pianist. He wrote *Peer Gynt* in 1875, which contains the well-known melodies from *Morning Mood* and *In the Hall of the Mountain King.*

LITERATURE

The same year Grieg completed *Morning Mood,* French author Jules Verne published *Twenty Thousand Leagues Under the Sea.* This science fiction novel tells the story of Captain Nemo and his adventures aboard the submarine *Nautilus.*

WORLD

The first transcontinental railroad line was completed in the United States, joining the lines being built from Omaha, Nebraska and Sacramento, California.

2.21 MORNING MOOD

Edvard Grieg

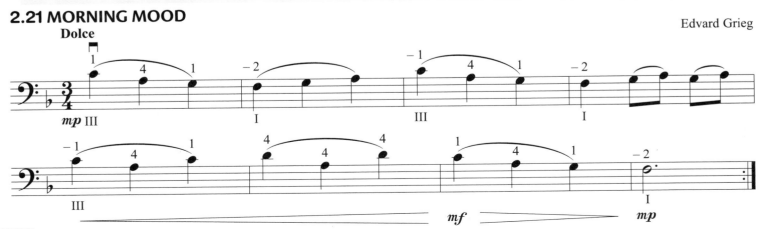

On this page, you learn **B-flat in 1st position**. Once you have practiced these pieces, you can move to page 17b where you will learn half position. On page 17c, you have the opportunity to play these same pieces using B-flat in half position.

NEW NOTE: B♭ (B-FLAT)
B♭ is played with 2 fingers on the G string in 1st position.

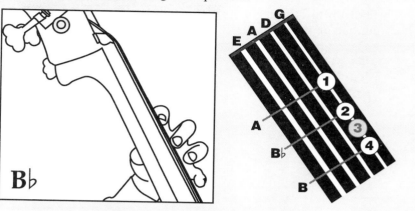

2.22 I'M FLAT-TERED

2.23 SNEAKY STARS

French Melody Adaptation

ACCENT
> An **accent** indicates to emphasize a note by playing louder.
Sink the weight of the bow into the string and move the bow quickly!

2.24 PRELUDE FOR A PRINCE

2.24a ONE WAY OR ANOTHER - Bass only *Practice playing F natural in 2nd position.*

2.25 PRINCE OF DENMARK'S MARCH
When you have an up bow on an accent, be sure that your right thumb is bent as you sink your arm weight into the string.

Jeremiah Clarke

SB308DB

SHIFTING

FINDING HALF POSITION

To play in **half position**, shift your left hand toward the nut so that your 2nd finger moves
to A on the G string. Make sure your thumb moves with your hand, staying relaxed and opposite
your 2nd finger. You can now play B♭ with your 4th finger.

A is played with 2 fingers in
half position on the G string.

B♭ is played with 4 fingers in
half position on the G string.

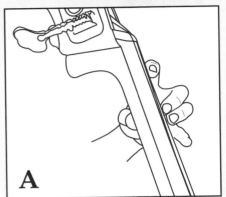

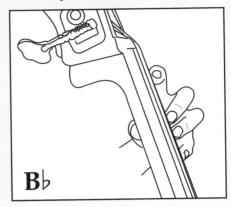

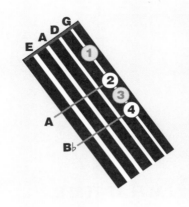

2.25a GLASS HALF FULL - Bass only

2.25b GLASS HALF EMPTY - Bass only

HALF POSITION ON THE D STRING

The following two exercises will help you become familiar
with using half position on the D string.

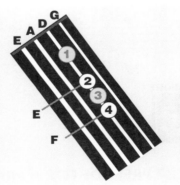

2.25c HALF COUSINS - Bass only

2.25d THEME FROM SYMPHONY NO. 1 - Bass only

Gustav Mahler

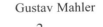

On this page, you play **B-flat in half position**. Make sure you have already practiced page 17a, which has the same pieces but uses B-flat in 1st position.

2.22 I'M FLAT-TERED

2.23 SNEAKY STARS

French Melody Adaptation

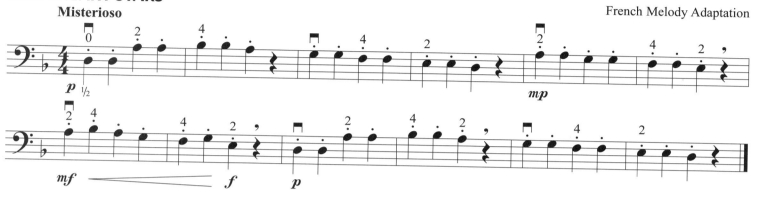

ACCENT

> An **accent** indicates to emphasize a note by playing louder.
Sink the weight of the bow into the string and move the bow quickly!

2.24 PRELUDE FOR A PRINCE

2.25 PRINCE OF DENMARK'S MARCH

When you have an up bow on an accent, be sure that your right thumb is bent as you sink your arm weight into the string.

Jeremiah Clarke

HISTORY

MUSIC

Austrian composer **Franz Joseph Haydn** (1732–1809) is often referred to as the father of the symphony (he wrote 108 of them!). Brahms discovered Haydn's *Chorale St. Antoni,* which was originally scored as a wind ensemble piece.

LITERATURE

Phillis Wheatley became the first published African-American woman (and only the second published African-American poet). She was popular in both England and in the American colonies.

WORLD

The United States *Bill of Rights* was ratified and became the first ten amendments to the Constitution. It guaranteed certain personal freedoms and placed limits on the power of government.

2.26 SAINT ANTHONY'S CHORALE

Franz Joseph Haydn

NEW NOTE: B-FLAT

B♭ is played with 1st finger on the A string in half position.

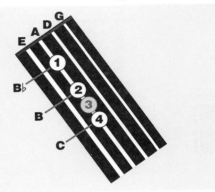

2.27 APPROACH FROM ABOVE

2.28 LAMB ABOVE, LAMB BELOW

Traditional Adaptation

2.29 GOLDEN SLIPPERS

James A. Bland

SHIFTING

19

NEW NOTE: F

F is played with 1st finger on the E string in half position.
Notice you can also play G with 4 fingers on the E string in half position.

2.30 NEW FRONTIERS

NEW NOTE! F

2.31 F MAJOR SCALE

2.32 WHO CAN SAIL WITHOUT THE WIND

Swedish Folk Song

2.33 COMING TO AMERICA

2.34 AMERICA

Traditional

Stately

2.35 TO BE OR NOT TO B-FLAT?

2.36 INTENTIONAL ACCIDENTAL POLKA

Allegro

SB308DB

RHYTHM

EIGHTH RESTS

The **eighth rest** receives one-half of a beat in $\frac{4}{4}$ time.

Eighth rests can replace upbeat eighth notes. Eighth rests can replace downbeat eighth notes.

2.37 BOW BEAT *Notice how measures 2 and 3 should sound the same!*

2.38 EIGHTH TIME'S A CHARM *Always remember to check the key signature!*

2.39 THE RAKES OF MALLOW

Irish Folk Song

2.40 BOW BEAT

2.41 OFF TOPIC

2.42 B-I-(N)-G-O

English Folk Song

INTERPRETATION STATION

Listen to the corresponding track on the DVD. You will hear four examples. Listen to the bowing and decide whether the example illustrates detaché, staccato or accents. D - detaché   S - staccato   A - accent

1. _____   2. _____   3. _____   4. _____

SIMON SEZ

Listen to the corresponding track on the DVD. You will hear a series of one-measure patterns that only use open strings. Listen carefully to the bowing, then echo them back, matching the articulations you hear.

COMPOSER'S CORNER

Write a melody for this duet. Pair up with a friend and perform it for your class or family! Before composing, play the B line first to get the sound in your ear. Then think about the melody.

PENCIL POWER

These four musical examples are missing rests! Fill in the shaded boxes with quarter and eighth rests to complete the measure. Be sure to check the time signature!

1.

2.

3.

4.

CURTAIN UP!

2.43 COVENTRY CAROL

English Carol

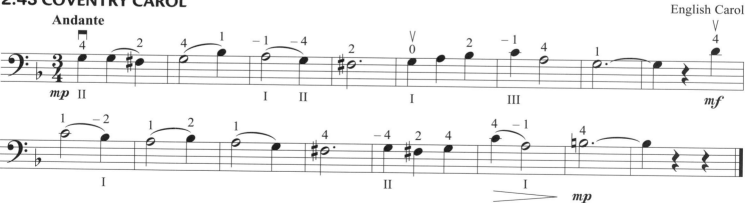

BOW-NUS!

2.44 CUCKOO GONE CUCKOO *Practice playing staccatos, accents, and detaché. Watch for the harmonic in measure 4!*

CURTAIN UP!

2.45 STILL WATERS - Orchestra Arrangement

Brian Balmages

3.1 FINGER STRETCHER - Duet
Take turns playing the A and B parts. Listen carefully to be sure your notes are in tune with the other part!

3.2 SHARP SEA SHARKS

3.3 AU CLAIRE DE LA LUNE

French Folk Song

SECOND POSITION ON THE A STRING

Using second position on the A string allows you to play C♯ with 2 fingers and D with 4 fingers. Remember to keep your thumb relaxed and opposite finger 2 when you shift.

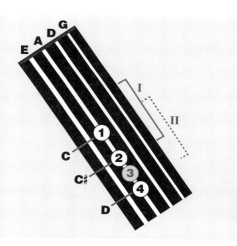

3.4 EIGHTH NOTE GALOP

Presto *(very quickly)*

3.5 GO TELL AUNT RHODY

American Folk Song

3.6 GOOD KING WENCESLAS

English Carol

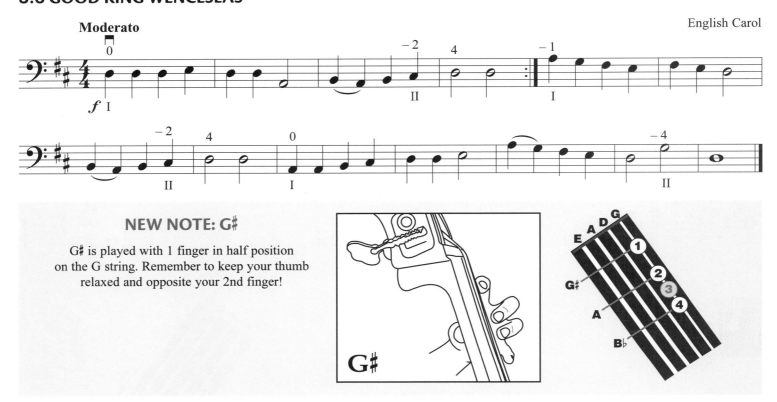

NEW NOTE: G♯

G♯ is played with 1 finger in half position on the G string. Remember to keep your thumb relaxed and opposite your 2nd finger!

3.7 FINGER TWINS

3.8 BACKYARD BOOGIE

3.9 PARALLEL THEMES

NEW KEY SIGNATURE

This is the key of **A Major.**  This key signature indicates that F, C, and G should be played as F-sharp, C-sharp and G-sharp.

3.10 2nd VERSE, SAME AS THE 1st!

3.11 A MAJOR SCALE

3.12 ARIRANG

Korean Folk Song

3.13 AURA LEE

American Folk Song

3.14 OBWISANA

Ghanian Folk Song

SB308DB

3.15 BELLS FOR BELLINI

3.16 SUMMER'S END

HISTORY

MUSIC
Italian composer **Antonio Vivaldi** (1678–1741) wrote in the Baroque Period. He was an excellent violinist and wrote numerous concertos. *Autumn* is from a set of violin concertos called *The Four Seasons*. Each movement represented a season of the year.

LITERATURE
The year after *The Four Seasons* was published, Jonathan Swift completed *Gulliver's Travels*. The novel is an excellent example of Swift as a master of satire and parody.

WORLD
The Treaty of Seville (1729) ended the Anglo-Spanish War, which involved Great Britain, France and Spain. The Comet of 1729 was discovered by Nicolas Sarabat and is still considered to be one of the largest comets ever seen.

3.17 AUTUMN FROM THE FOUR SEASONS - Duet

Antonio Vivaldi

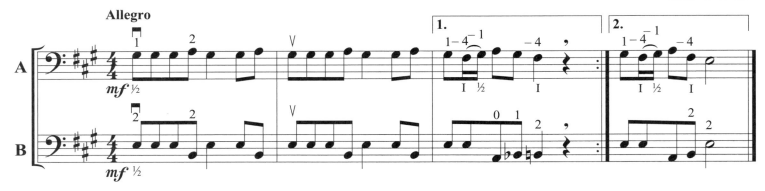

3.18 ALL THROUGH THE NIGHT *Notice the hooked bowing in measure 3.*

Welsh Folk Song

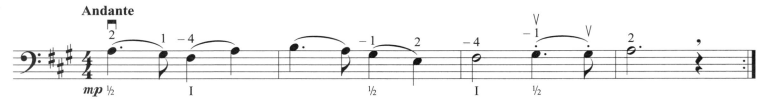

3.19 DOTS AND HOOKS
Practice playing multiple hooked bowings with dotted rhythms.
Notice the key signature of G Major, which indicates G and C natural!

HISTORY

MUSIC

Giuseppe Verdi (1813–1901) was an Italian composer best known for his operas, especially *Il Trovatore*. The *Anvil Chorus* comes from Act 2 and features Spanish gypsies who sing and strike anvils as they work in the early morning.

LITERATURE

Harriet Beecher Stowe's novel *Uncle Tom's Cabin* was published in 1852. It is arguably one of the most influential publications in the history of American society as it helped cement the opposition to slavery in the North.

WORLD

The Crimean War began in 1853. Also known as the Russo-Turkish War, it involved Russia and the Ottomans. France and Great Britain sided with the Ottomans and also declared war on Russia.

3.20 ANVIL CHORUS
Giuseppe Verdi

3.21 LITTLE SWALLOW
Chinese Folk Song

3.22 PRELUDE TO TE DEUM
Marc-Antoine Charpentier

SB308DB

RHYTHM

DOTTED EIGHTH NOTE/SIXTEENTH NOTE GROUP
Adding a dot after a note increases the length of the note by half of its value.
Here the dot is used with an eighth note to create a **dotted eighth note.**

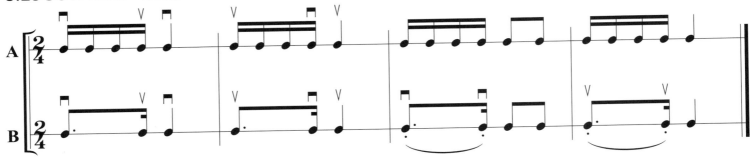

3.23 BOW BEAT - Duet

3.24 LINE (UP) DANCE - Duet

3.25 O TANNENBAUM
Use enough bow on the dotted eighth and sixteenth notes so you have enough bow for beats 2 and 3.

German Folk Song

3.26 UN-FINISHING TOUCHES

HISTORY

MUSIC
Franz Schubert (1797–1828) had only completed two movements of his *Symphony No. 8* before he abandoned it. Nicknamed "The Unfinished," it ironically contains one of the most famous themes known to the world today.

LITERATURE
English author Mary Shelley brought the name "Frankenstein" to life in her novel by the same name. Written in the midst of the Gothic and Romantic Literary Periods, it is also considered to be one of the earliest examples of science fiction.

WORLD
Three different captains confirmed a sighting of Antarctica in 1820. Despite the numerous ice formations on its coast, Antarctica is considered to be a desert due to limited precipitation.

3.27 THEME FROM SYMPHONY NO. 8 *Start in the middle of the bow so you have enough bow for measure 2.* — Franz Schubert

This is the sym-pho-ny that Schu-bert wrote but nev-er fin-ished!

SHIFTING

FINDING FOURTH POSITION - Bass only

To play in **fourth position**, shift your left hand so that your first finger moves to D on the G string. Remember to keep your thumb relaxed. It will sit in the curve of the neck.

D is played with 1 finger in IV position on the G string

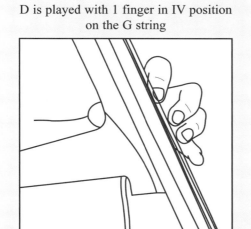
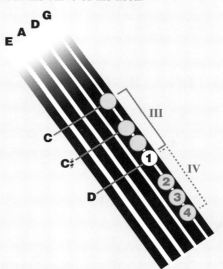

The following exercises will help you become comfortable with playing in IV position.

3.27a FOUR SCORE - Bass only

3.27b THREE TO FOUR - Bass only

SB308DB

IV POSITION ON THE D STRING

IV POSITION ON THE A STRING

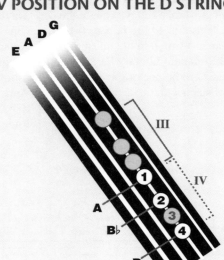

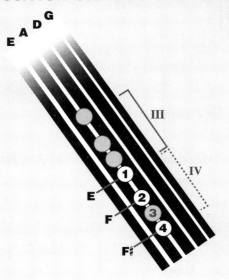

3.27c FOURTH ON D - Bass only

3.27d FOURTH ON D AND G, SEE? - Bass only

3.27e FOURTH ON A - Bass only

3.27f MORE FOUR - Bass only   *Notice how you can play this entire piece in IV position.*

THIRD AND A HALF (III ¹/₂) POSITION

To play in **third and a half position**, shift your left hand so that your 1st finger moves to C♯ on the G string. Remember that your thumb should also move, staying behind your 2nd finger. This makes it easy to play C♯ when coming from fourth position.

3.27g HALF PLUS THREE ON G - Bass only

SB308DB

NEW NOTE: E

E is played with 4 fingers in IV position on the G string.

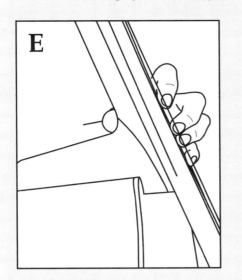

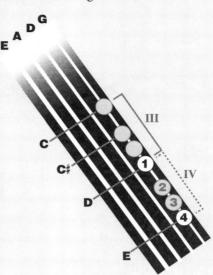

3.28 POSITIONED TO SUCCEED

3.29 AIKEN DRUM
Practice counting and singing the upbeats in this piece before you play.
Notice that you are only shifting the distance of a half step.

Scottish Folk Song

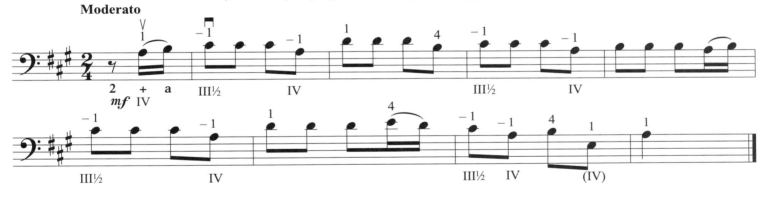

3.30 KANGDING LOVE SONG
Play this entire piece in IV position.

Chinese Folk Song

30

THEORY

TENUTO AND STACCATO

Tenuto
Play with full value and stress each note.

Staccato
Play light and separated.

3.31 DONNA'S SONG

3.32 MOBILE MELODY

3.33 LA DONNA É MOBILE
Giuseppe Verdi

HISTORY

MUSIC

Richard Wagner (1813–1883) was a German composer who is best known for his operas. His opera *Lohengrin* tells the story of a mysterious knight who is eventually forced to reveal his true amazing identity to the King. The *Bridal Chorus* is the most well-known theme in the opera.

LITERATURE

French author Victor Hugo completed *Les Miserables,* a novel about the French rebellion that culminates in the Paris Uprising of 1832. It remains extremely popular to this day and has been adapted for film, musical theater and television.

WORLD

Charles Darwin set forth his theory of evolution and the process of natural selection. His publication *The Origin of Species* became the foundation of evolutionary biology.

3.34 BRIDAL CHORUS FROM LOHENGRIN
Richard Wagner

SYNCOPATION

You already know the quarter-half-quarter syncopation. The most common syncopated rhythm is eighth-quarter-eighth. Here the syncopation occurs on the accented upbeat quarter note.

3.35 BOW BEAT

3.36 IN SYNC-OPATION

3.37 BOW BEAT

3.38 HOOK, LINE AND SYNCOPATION

3.39 LI'L LIZA JANE *Play in the middle of the bow for mezzo forte and closer to the frog for forte!*

American Folk Song

3.40 ON A ROLL

3.41 CAISSON SONG

Edmund L. Gruber

SB308DB

OPUS 3 ENCORE

INTERPRETATION STATION

Listen to the corresponding track on the DVD. You will hear four examples. For each one, decide if the articulation is **Legato** or **Staccato**. Circle the letter that corresponds with your answer.

1. L S   2. L S   3. L S   4. L S

SIMON SEZ

Listen to the corresponding track on the DVD. You will hear a familiar song. Listen first, sing it, then find the pitches on your instrument. You can then play along with the accompaniment track that follows!

COMPOSER'S CORNER

Writing a theme is just one part of a composer's process. Composers also use dynamics to make their music more expressive. Add your own dynamics and bowings to make this piece expressive. Choose from the following:

PENCIL POWER

Match the composer with the correct fact by writing in the appropriate letter.

1. ____ Antonio Vivaldi	**A.** Italian composer best known for his operas
2. ____ Richard Wagner	**B.** German composer best known for his operas and the popular wedding music that came from his opera *Lohengrin*
3. ____ Edvard Grieg	**C.** German composer who was also an accomplished pianist
4. ____ Franz Schubert	**D.** Czech composer known for his *Symphony No. 9* (*"From the New World"*)
5. ____ Johannes Brahms	**E.** Austrian composer well-known for a famous theme from a symphony that he never finished
6. ____ Franz Joseph Haydn	**F.** Norwegian composer who wrote *In the Hall of the Mountain King*
7. ____ Giuseppe Verdi	**G.** Austrian composer who is often referred to as the father of the symphony
8. ____ Antonín Dvořák	**H.** Italian composer who wrote numerous concertos in the Baroque Period including *The Four Seasons*

CURTAIN UP!

3.42 MIXING BOWL MARCH

BOW-NUS!

3.43 ARRR-MONIC! *Imagine yourself on a pirate ship while playing this piece!*

CURTAIN UP!

3.44 ENTRY OF THE WARRIORS - Orchestra Arrangement *A **fermata** (⌢) means to hold a note longer than its value. Watch your conductor!*

Brian Balmages

OPUS 4

RHYTHM

MORE TIME SIGNATURES

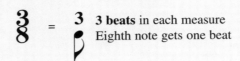

$\frac{3}{8}$ = 3 **3 beats** in each measure
Eighth note gets one beat

4.1 BOW BEAT - Duet

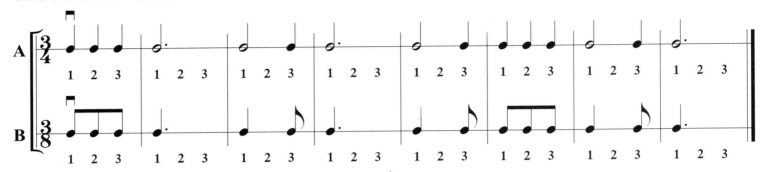

4.2 D IN THREE

4.3 THREE-EIGHTH'S FRENCH - Duet

French Folk Song

4.4 WE THREE KINGS

John H. Hopkins Jr.

Andante

MORE TIME SIGNATURES

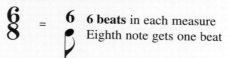

$\frac{6}{8}$ = **6** **6 beats** in each measure
Eighth note gets one beat

In a faster tempo, emphasis is often placed on the 1st and 4th beats of each measure.
This gives the music a strong 2-beat pulse.

4.5 BOW BEAT

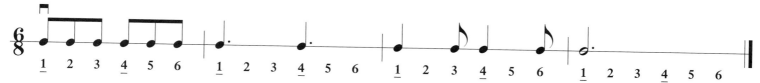

4.6 ODE TO 6/8

4.7 GETTING THE HOOK OF IT

4.8 LOOBY LOO

Traditional

Moderato

4.9 POP! GOES THE WEASEL *Did you find the left-hand pizzicato in measure 7?*

English Traditional

Playful

SB308DB

36

4.10 ITALIAN PRELUDE *Look at your key signature before you begin. What fingerings will you be using?*

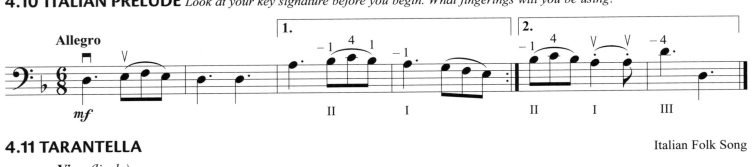

4.11 TARANTELLA

Italian Folk Song

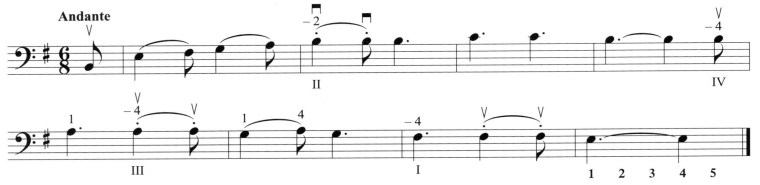

4.12 THEME FROM THE MOLDAU

Bedřich Smetana

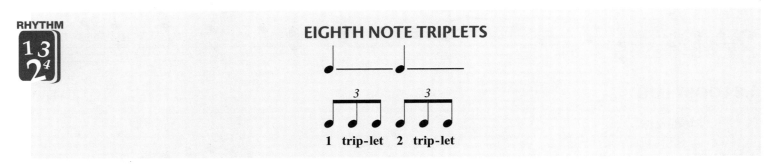

RHYTHM 13 2/4

EIGHTH NOTE TRIPLETS

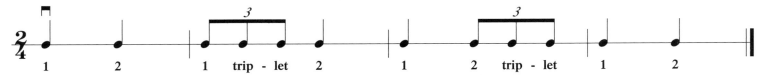

1 trip-let 2 trip-let

4.13 BOW BEAT

1 2 1 trip - let 2 1 2 trip - let 1 2

4.14 TRIPLE HEADER

1 2 1 trip - let 2 III 1 2 trip - let 1 2

SB308DB

4.15 NIGHT ON BALD MOUNTAIN

Modest Mussorgsky

Pesante

ff *(fortissimo - louder than forte)*

4.16 SAILING WITH COLUMBUS

4.17 FINALE FROM SYMPHONY NO. 9

Antonín Dvořák

Allegro con fuoco *(fast, with fiery energy)*

NEW NOTE: E♭

E♭ is played with 1 finger in half position on the D string. Remember to keep your thumb relaxed and opposite your 2nd finger!

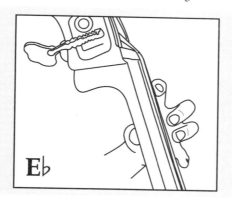

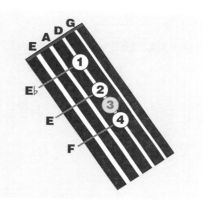

4.18 A PENTATONIC THEME

NEW NOTE! E♭

4.19 WACKY RHODY

Adaptation

SB308DB

4.20 BE FLAT

THEORY

NEW KEY SIGNATURE

 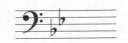

This is the key of
B♭ Major.

This key signature indicates that all Bs and
Es should be played as B-flats and E-flats.

4.21 B♭ MAJOR SCALE

4.22 LONDON BRIDGE

English Folk Song

4.23 SAKURA, SAKURA - Duet

Japanese Folk Song

4.24 O CANADA

Canadian National Anthem 39
Calixa Lavallée, Sir Adolphe-Basile Routhier, and Justice R.S. Weir

MUSIC
Gustav Holst (1874–1934) was an English composer best known for his orchestral suite *The Planets* and the two most performed movements: *Mars and Jupiter.* He is also well-known for his two suites for band, which are considered cornerstones of the repertoire.

LITERATURE
American author L. Frank Baum introduced the world to Dorothy in his novel *The Wonderful Wizard of Oz.* English author Frances Hodgson Burnett wrote *The Secret Garden,* which became a very popular children's novel.

WORLD
Time magazine was first published in 1923. The world got a lot sweeter with the invention of *Reese's® Peanut Butter Cups, Butterfinger®,* and *Milky Way®* bars!

4.25 IN THE BLEAK MIDWINTER

Gustav Holst

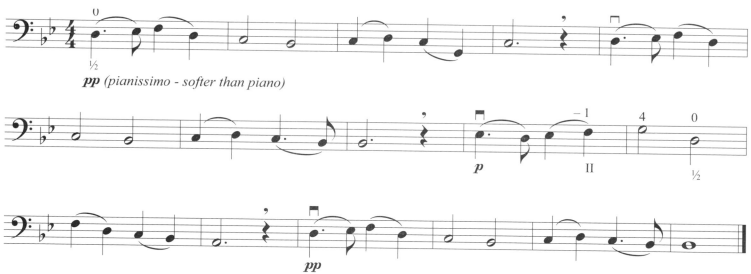

SB308DB

4.26 LULLABY

4.27 SKIPPING ALONG

4.28 WALTZ OF THE FLAT BEES

4.29 HUNGARIAN DANCE NO. 5

Johannes Brahms

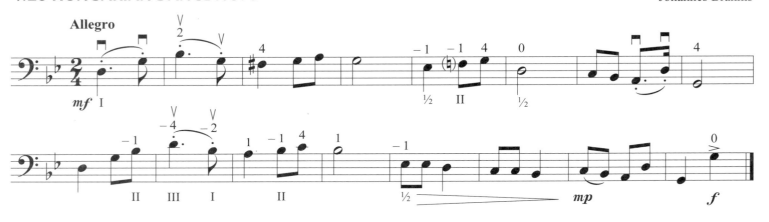

4.30 BY THE WATERS OF BABYLON - Round

Philip Hayes

Andante

RHYTHM 13

METER CHANGES

You have already played pieces with variations that use a meter change. Sometimes the meter can change within the main melody.

- Look ahead as you play.
- Check each time signature to determine how many beats are in each measure and what kind of note gets one beat.

HISTORY

MUSIC

Modest Mussorgsky (1839–1881) was a Russian composer famous for works including *Night on Bald Mountain* (on page 37 of this book!) and his *Pictures at an Exhibition*. The *Promenade* resembles Russian folk music with strong rhythms and asymmetrical meter (changing time signatures).

LITERATURE

The 1850s saw the completion of two major American novels. Nathaniel Hawthorne wrote *The Scarlet Letter* and a year later, Herman Melville completed his epic tale of *Moby Dick*.

WORLD

The year after Mussorgsky completed *Pictures at an Exhibition,* the Civil Rights Act of 1875 was passed in the United States. It was a big step toward the establishment of equal rights regardless of skin color.

4.31 PROMENADE FROM PICTURES AT AN EXHIBITION

Modest Mussorgsky

4.32 THE FIVE DAYS OF STRING CLASS

Traditional English Melody

On the fifth day of string class, my teach - er gave to me:

five notes to learn! Four___ brand new strings, three les - sons,

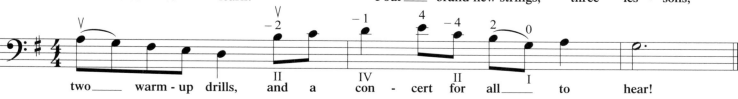

two___ warm - up drills, and a con - cert for all___ to hear!

SB308DB

42

THEORY

ENHARMONICS

Two notes that have the same pitch but different names are called **enharmonics**. An example would be E♭ and D♯.
They have different names but share the same fingering and sound the same when played!

4.33 SOUND-A-LIKES *Be sure your thumb stays opposite your 2nd finger as you move into and out of half position.*

4.34 A MINOR MELODY

RHYTHM 13

CUT TIME (ALLA BREVE)

$$\mathbf{C} = \frac{2}{2} = \begin{matrix} 2 \\ \circ \end{matrix}$$ 2 beats in each measure.
Half note gets one beat.

4.35 BOW BEAT - Duet

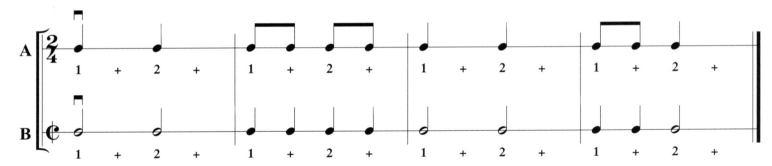

4.36 CUT IT OUT

4.37 MARCH OF THE SCISSORS

SB308DB

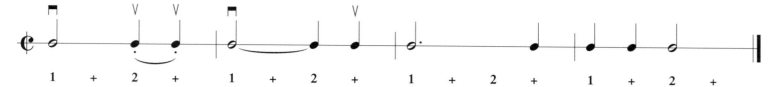

4.38 BOW BEAT

4.39 CUT ALONG THE DOTS

4.40 BOW BEAT

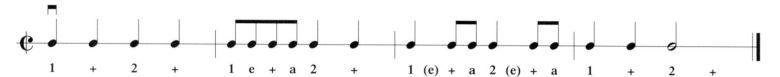

4.41 HOME WITH LOU

4.42 SKIP TO MY LOU

American Folk Song

4.43 MARCH OF THE METAL MEN

Leon Jessel

4.44 PARADE OF THE WOODEN SOLDIERS

Notice that the entire piece is in IV position except for the C♯s, which are a half step lower in III¹⁄₂ position.

Leon Jessel

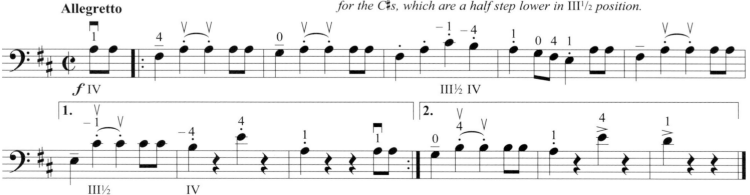

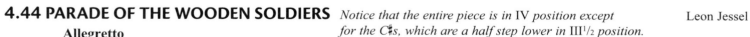

OPUS 4 ENCORE

INTERPRETATION STATION

Listen to the corresponding track on the DVD. You will hear four musical examples, all composed using a different time signature. As you listen, pay close attention to how rhythmic ideas are grouped. Circle the correct time signature for each example.

1. $\frac{6}{8}$ $\math3\2$ 2. $\frac{4}{4}$ $\frac{3}{8}$ 3. $\frac{3}{4}$ $\mathC$ 4. $\frac{2}{4}$ $\frac{3}{8}$

SIMON SEZ

Listen to the corresponding track on the DVD. You will hear a familiar song. Listen first, sing it, then find the pitches on your instrument. You can then play along with the accompaniment track that follows!

COMPOSER'S CORNER

It is time for you to put together everything you have learned and compose your own piece! First, decide what key you want the piece to be in. Next, choose a time signature. Finally, compose your own 4-measure melody and add dynamics and bowings. Play it for a friend or family member. Remember: you can *always* change something after you hear it!

Title: _____   Composer: _____

PENCIL POWER

Match the composer with the correct fact by writing in the appropriate letter.

1. _____ Accent   5. _____ Tenuto
2. _____ Prelude   6. _____ Allegro con fuoco
3. _____ Vivo   7. _____ Largo
4. _____ Enharmonics   8. _____ Marziale

A. Fast, with fiery energy
B. A piece of music that introduces a larger work
C. A lively tempo
D. March tempo
E. A slow, solemn tempo
F. Two notes that have the same pitch but different names.
G. Play full value and stress each note
H. Emphasize a note by playing louder

CURTAIN UP!

4.45 BLOW THE MAN DOWN

Sea Shanty

BOW-NUS!

4.46 CREEPY CRAWLY

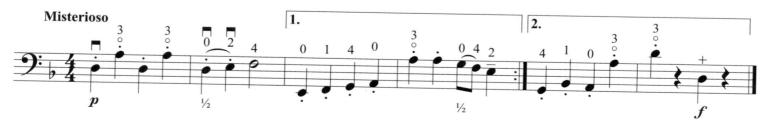

4.47 DANCE OF THE GREMLINS - Orchestra Arrangement

Brian Balmages

SB308DB

CODA: AN INTRODUCTION TO SHIFTING

Up until now, most of the other string players have been playing in 1st position. They now begin to practice playing in 3rd position. This is also an excellent opportunity to do some additional shifting exercises for bass.

5.1 THE RAIN WENT AWAY *Keep your 1st finger in contact with the string when you shift.*

Adaptation

5.2 LULLABY-ISH *Your thumb should stay relaxed and behind your 2nd finger when you shift.*

Adaptation

5.3 E-I-E-I-O SINGS MARY

Traditional

5.4 FEELING SHIFTY

5.5 SHIFTIN' HOME

Antonín Dvořák

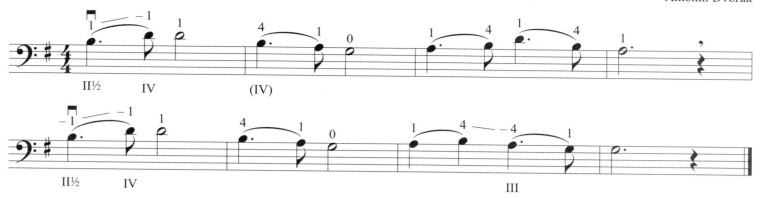

SCALES AND ARPEGGIOS

D MAJOR

G MAJOR

C MAJOR

F MAJOR

A MAJOR

B♭ MAJOR

E MAJOR

SB308DB

INDEX